JB
LAW~~RENCE~~
BUR

W9-AAZ-549

SIZZLING

Celebrities

Jennifer!

FILM STAR
JENNIFER LAWRENCE

BY JEFF BURLINGAME

Enslow Publishers, Inc.
40 Industrial Road
Box 398
Berkeley Heights, NJ 07922
USA
http://www.enslow.com

Copyright © 2014 by Enslow Publishers, Inc.

All rights reserved.

No part of this book may be reproduced by any means without the written permission of the publisher.

Library of Congress Cataloging-in-Publication Data:

Burlingame, Jeff.

  Jennifer! : film star Jennifer Lawrence / Jeff Burlingame.
  pages cm. — (Sizzling celebrities)
  Summary: "Read about Jennifer's early life, how she got started in acting, and her future plans"—Provided by publisher.
  ISBN 978-0-7660-4170-7
  1. Lawrence, Jennifer, 1990—Juvenile literature. 2. Actors—United States—Biography—Juvenile literature. I. Title.
  PN2287.L28948B87 2014
  791.4302'8092—dc23
  [B]   2012040315

Future editions:
Paperback ISBN: 978-1-4644-0279-1
EPUB ISBN: 978-1-4645-1176-9
Single-User PDF ISBN: 978-1-4646-1176-6
Multi-User PDF ISBN: 978-0-7660-5805-7

Printed in the United States of America

052013 Lake Book Manufacturing, Inc., Melrose Park, IL

10 9 8 7 6 5 4 3 2 1

To Our Readers: We have done our best to make sure all Internet addresses in this book were active and appropriate when we went to press. However, the author and the publisher have no control over and assume no liability for the material available on those Internet sites or on other Web sites they may link to. Any comments or suggestions can be sent by e-mail to comments@enslow.com or to the address on the back cover.

♻ Enslow Publishers, Inc., is committed to printing our books on recycled paper. The paper in every book contains 10% to 30% post-consumer waste (PCW). The cover board on the outside of each book contains 100% PCW. Our goal is to do our part to help young people and the environment too!

Photo Credits: AP Photo/Brian Bohannon, p. 11; AP Photo/Carlo Allegri, p. 29; AP Photo/Charles Sykes, pp. 39, 42, 46; AP Photo/Chris Allegri, p. 6; AP Photo/Chris Pizzello, pp. 9, 23; AP Photo/David J. Philip, p. 13; AP Photo/Evan Agostini, pp. 34, 45; AP Photo/Franz Neumayr, p. 15; AP Photo/Jae C. Hong, p. 33; AP Photo/Jennifer Graylock, p. 41; AP Photo/Joel Ryan, pp. 10, 35; AP Photo/Julio Ortez, p. 17; AP Photo/Katy Winn, p. 38; AP Photo/Matt Sayles, pp. 4, 7, 30; AP Photo/Peter Kramer, p. 24; AP Photo/Richard Drew, p. 21; John Shearer/Invision/AP, p. 1.

Cover Photo: John Shearer/Invision/AP (Jennifer Lawrence poses with her Oscar for Best Actress at the 85th Academy Awards ceremony.)

Contents

CHAPTER 1
Academy Award Nominee, 5

CHAPTER 2
Her Old Kentucky Home, 11

CHAPTER 3
Rising Star, 20

CHAPTER 4
Blockbusters, 32

CHAPTER 5
Academy Award Winner, 44

Further Info, 47
Index, 48

7

Academy Award Nominee

Jennifer Lawrence wasn't as well known as her competition. In fact, she wasn't as well known as most of those seated around her. Yet there she was on February 27, 2011, at the Kodak Theatre in Hollywood, California. She was watching in person as some of the biggest movie stars in the world were honored at the Academy Awards. It was a dream come true.

The reason Jennifer was there was the best part of the story. She wasn't there as a fan who was simply happy to be among the best actors and actresses alive. She was at the Academy Awards—which are also known as the Oscars—because she was one of the best actors and actresses alive. She had earned that title one month earlier when she was nominated for the Best Actress award for her role in the independent movie *Winter's Bone*.

At twenty years old, Jennifer was by far the youngest and least experienced of the five nominees for Best Actress. The others

◀ *Jennifer Lawrence arrives at Academy Awards on February 27, 2011.*

▲ Jennifer Lawrence (back row, fourth from left) poses with the rest of the cast of Winter's Bone.

included film veterans Annette Bening, Nicole Kidman, Natalie Portman, and Michelle Williams. Jennifer told *Entertainment Weekly*, "I honestly feel like I'm in the same category and the same sentence with actresses I've been looking up to for most of my career. ... I reeeaaally don't care [if I win]. I really am just happy to be nominated."

Just by being nominated, Jennifer had almost set a record. She was the second-youngest person ever nominated for Best Actress. She told one reporter from *Louisville Magazine* that every time someone asked her about the Oscars, "I put my fingers in my ears and go 'la-la-la-la-la' every time I hear that word. I have no idea how to talk about an Oscar at twenty years old. I can, like, make a dentist appointment, barely. I don't even know how to shop online."

Not many people believed Jennifer stood a chance of winning the Academy Award. She didn't think she had

Natalie Portman was ▶ *pregnant when she beat out Jennifer Lawrence for the Academy Award for Best Actress.*

a shot, either. In fact, Jennifer admitted she spent some time practicing the face she was going to make for the TV cameras when she lost. Walking the red carpet before the ceremony in a red Calvin Klein dress, she told a *TV Guide* reporter, "I really am just totally happy to be here. I can't wait to use my losing face."

Jennifer got to use that losing face near the end of the show, when Portman won the award. As it turns out, her losing face was a toothy smile she wore the whole time Portman made her way to the stage. Despite Jennifer's declaration that her face was planned, it didn't look like she was faking it. It looked like she really was happy, and she had every reason to be. She knew that being nominated for such a huge award would do wonders for her career. And it did. It gave her opportunities to audition for (and win!) starring roles in some of the biggest movies being made, including *X-Men: First Class* and *The Hunger Games*. It took her from being a virtually unknown actress to the top of the A-list. The world now knew her as Jennifer Lawrence, Academy Award nominee. She was a rising star.

Jennifer said she wouldn't let any of her new attention go to her head. She told the *Wall Street Journal*, "Being an actress is such a tiny part of what I want to be. I want to make films … and I want to be an actress like Meryl Streep and I want to be a mom like mine and drive a minivan."

Actors and actresses often struggle for decades to get a break as big as Jennifer's. Most of them never get one. Jennifer's big break was her Academy Award nomination. She received it

Jennifer Lawrence hangs out with fellow Oscar nominee Hailee Steinfeld at the Governor's Ball following the Academy Awards.

Meryl Streep is an inspiration for Jennifer Lawrence. Streep won the Academy Award for Best Actress in 2012. Here she poses with Jean Dujardin, who won the award for Best Actor.

just six years after she began acting professionally. But that didn't mean she got lucky. Jennifer used hard work, talent, and determination to become a great actress so quickly. And she did it all beginning in the most unlikely of places.

Her Old Kentucky Home

Jennifer Shrader Lawrence was born far away from the bright lights of Hollywood on August 15, 1990, in Louisville, Kentucky. Louisville is the largest city in the state and nicknamed Derby City. It's called that because every May, the popular Kentucky Derby horse race is held there at a world-famous track called Churchill Downs.

Jennifer grew up in Louisville, Kentucky.

Jennifer did not have any horses of her own when she was growing up, but she did have a pet goat and several family dogs. She also had two older brothers, Ben and Blaine. Just as many older brothers do to younger siblings, Ben and Blaine used to tease Jennifer at every opportunity.

Jennifer's family lived in a large, tidy, red-brick house in the prosperous Louisville suburb of Indian Hills. Her father, Gary, owned a concrete business, and her mother, Karen, was a former cheerleader at the University of Louisville who ran a summer day camp for kids called Hi-Ho.

As might be expected of a young girl with two older brothers— and one whose grandfather had been a basketball star at the University of Kentucky —Jennifer grew up a tomboy. She was even nicknamed Nitro because she was so hyper. She played tennis, field hockey, and softball. Like many Kentuckians, she also developed an early love of horses. Jennifer told *Seventeen* magazine, "I lived 15 minutes away from a horse farm, and I went there almost every day. My brothers were into fishing, but I was all about the horses."

Finding Her Passion

The tall, blonde-haired, blue-eyed girl also had a feminine side. She was a cheerleader in school just as her mother had been. She also modeled and acted in plays at Christ Methodist Church and at the Walden Theatre in Louisville. When she was in junior high school, Jennifer spent a semester

Since the Kentucky Derby is held in Jennifer Lawrence's home state, horseback riding became a popular hobby for her.

at Walden learning acting basics. One early highlight was the time she played a woman named Desdemona in a scene from Shakespeare's *Othello*. Her mother later told separate interviewers, "That's the only time I can say she really loved something and connected with it," and "In our family, everything was about sports. If she could've thrown a baseball, we would have been able to tell that she could pitch. We just didn't recognize her talent."

Jennifer's acting talent was obvious to those who worked with young actors and actresses. She was also far more determined to succeed at acting—or anything she attempted—than most kids her age. Her acting teacher at the Walden Theatre told the *Daily Mail*, "She was inquisitive, eager, and attentive in class. I remember she did a scene from *Othello* and she picked it up very quickly. She learned really quickly. I knew she was going to go places. ... We didn't get a lot of eighth-graders saying, 'I'm going to New York [to become a professional actress].' I got a sense that she was way more determined than most of the kids her age."

Jennifer was more mature than her peers in other ways, too. While many of her classmates at Kammerer Middle School struggled to accept their changing bodies, Jennifer had no problem dealing with hers. She said, "I remember when I was thirteen and it was cool to pretend to have an eating disorder because there were rumors that Lindsay Lohan and Nicole Richie were anorexic. I thought it was crazy. I went home and

One of Jennifer's first plays at the Walden Theatre was *Othello*. Above, Placido Domingo and Barbara Frittoli are in an opera version of the play.

told my mom, 'Nobody's eating bread—I just had to finish everyone's burgers.'"

In school, Jennifer walked a straight-and-narrow path that took her far from drugs and alcohol. She told *Teen Vogue* the biggest trouble she got into as a child was when she stuck gum underneath her living-room table. She said, "I didn't sneak out or drink. Once I told my parents to ground me because I was going to a party with alcohol. It's kind of disgusting."

Off to New York

Such maturity is what eventually helped persuade Jennifer's mom to take her to New York City to look into an acting career. They did so during spring break from school, when Jennifer was fourteen years old. Karen Lawrence said the trip was "to get this [strong desire to act] out of her system." Jennifer's mom didn't think much would come of the trip and that after making it, her daughter would begin to forget about being an actress.

At first, it looked like her mother was going to be correct. Jennifer met with a few modeling and acting agencies in New York, but nothing major came from the meetings. That is, until a man approached Jennifer and her mother while they were watching street dancers in busy Union Square. Jennifer told the *Courier-Journal*, "This guy was watching me, and he asked if he could take my picture. We didn't know that that was creepy, at the time. So we're like, 'Sure.' So he took my mom's phone number, and all of a sudden all these (modeling) agencies are calling. And that's when it all started." The picture-seeking man turned out to be a representative of the giant fashion company H&M. He had been out on the streets scouting talent for a future commercial when he spotted Jennifer.

Jennifer Lawrence took the plunge and moved to the much bigger city of New York in search of an acting career.

The phone calls continued when Jennifer and her mom returned to Kentucky. Eventually, Jennifer convinced her parents to let her move to New York for the summer. Her mom told *Louisville Magazine,* "We would have destroyed her had we not let her follow her dreams."

Jennifer still was only fourteen when she moved to New York, so her parents got her an apartment, and family members took turns staying with her while she went on casting calls. Jennifer later said that when she got to New York, "I just started getting an overwhelming feeling of being exactly where I needed to be exactly when I had to be there. Every time I would leave an agency and stop reading a script, I just wanted to keep going and going."

Jennifer's unique determination—and confidence—also shone through in New York. She worked hard and graduated high school two years early so she could concentrate on acting. Friends told her that by doing so she missed out on a lot of high school experiences, such as dances and sporting events. But Jennifer didn't think she missed much. In fact, she told the *Wall Street Journal,* "I wouldn't have been happy there. My mom always said that school changed me. I went from this happy kid to having anxiety problems. I used to get these crazy cramps. Everybody else could understand what was on the chalkboard but I felt so stupid the entire time I was in school." She told the *Los Angeles Times* that in school, "I always felt dumber than everybody else. I hated it. I hated being inside. I hated being behind a desk. School just kind of killed me."

Jennifer never felt stupid when she was acting. In fact, acting made her feel smart. She said she felt like she was finally succeeding at something. She told the *Los Angeles Times*, "I remember being in New York, reading a script and I completely understood it. I knew I could do it. ... They were offering me contracts on the spot and telling my mom I was good. I was finally hearing I was good at something. I didn't want to give up on that."

Jennifer's confidence began to soar. Once she found her passion for acting, she knew exactly what she was meant to do with her life and went after it with everything she had. She said, "I never considered that I wouldn't be successful. I never thought, 'If acting doesn't work out I can be a doctor.' The phrase 'If it doesn't work out' never popped into my mind. And that dumb determination of being a naive fourteen-year-old has never left me."

Rising Star

Jennifer's acting career was clearly on the rise by the time she turned fifteen in August 2005. Shortly after moving to New York, she had been cast in commercials for Verizon, Burger King, and MTV's *My Super Sweet 16*, in which she played a spoiled brat. In one *My Super Sweet 16* commercial, Jennifer can be seen lying on a table on which she is carried into her birthday party by four men. Then she is accidentally dumped off the table as she screams. Coincidentally, the MTV show premiered on August 15, which was Jennifer's real sixteenth birthday.

Jennifer also earned small roles in TV shows such as *Monk*, *Cold Case*, and *Medium*. Among her earliest highlights was landing a role in a made-for-TV movie called *Company Town*.

After she had been acting for a year, Jennifer landed her first major recurring role. It was on the TBS sitcom *The Bill Engvall Show*. Engvall was a successful stand-up comedian beginning his own TV series at the time. Jennifer was chosen to play Lauren Pearson, the daughter of the show's lead character.

Jennifer signed a seven-year contract with the show and eventually won a Young Artist Award for her acting.

The Bill Engvall Show was filmed in Los Angeles, which is where Jennifer and her family were now living. They had moved to California shortly before the show began to further Jennifer's

The actors who played Jennifer's parents on The Bill Engvall Show *were Bill Engvall and Nancy Travis.*

career. *The Bill Engvall Show* aired for three seasons before it was canceled by the network in 2009. By that time, Jennifer had realized she would like to do something bigger than television. She had decided she wanted to be a movie star. She told the *Courier-Journal*, "I love the show, and I love the people on it ... but if I had to turn down a movie for the show, I would die. That was always my biggest fear. ... I realized that I had an absolute passion for deep, dark indie movies." Indie, or independent, movies generally are produced with a much smaller budget than major motion pictures. Because of the lower cost, they often can take more risks in filming and don't have to appeal to as many people as major motion pictures do to break even. The storylines of indie films are often a little more quirky and artistic than major motion pictures.

Deep, Dark Movies

During the three years she was on *The Bill Engvall Show*, Lawrence spent her spare time dabbling in the deep, dark movies she found so alluring. She loved that style so much that she even turned down an offer to do a TV series with Disney because she didn't think she was the Disney type. By that, she meant she didn't want to play roles in humorous shows geared toward children. She wanted to play more serious parts.

Jennifer landed a small part in the drama *Garden Party* and a larger role alongside actress Selma Blair in *The Poker House*. In *The Poker House*, Jennifer plays Agnes, the oldest daughter of a drug-addicted mother living in a seedy home in a small Iowa

Jennifer Lawrence poses for a photo at the Turner Broadcasting upfronts. Upfronts are a way for TV channels to promote their new shows, such as The Bill Engvall Show.

town. The movie is based on the life of actress Lori Petty, who wrote and directed the film. A couple years after working on *The Poker House*, Jennifer told Collider.com, "Well, I was young. I hadn't done anything else and so everything that I read I wanted to do. But now that I'm older and actually have a point of view and I can see what an amazing, brilliant script [*The Poker House*] is and how it grabs you and it has teeth and it's real and it's ugly and all the things that aren't usually appealing really appeal to me."

Many people found Jennifer's acting in *The Poker House* appealing, including the judges at the Los Angeles Film Festival. They gave Jennifer an Outstanding Performance award for her work in the movie. It wasn't a major national

*Charlize Theron and Jennifer promote their movie
The Burning Plain.*

award, but Jennifer was happy to receive it. She saw it as
another step up the career ladder.

Both *Garden Party* and *The Poker House* were released in
2008. Another film Jennifer was in, *The Burning Plain*, was also
released then. The movie starred A-list actresses Charlize
Theron and Kim Basinger, and Jennifer has a large role in
it, too. The then-eighteen-year-old played Mariana, a dark

character who commits some twisted deeds, including killing birds with slingshots and then roasting them.

Critics felt *The Burning Plain* would be Jennifer's breakout role. It would be the one that would make her a household name. That led many media members to begin calling her the next big thing. But stardom didn't happen for Jennifer. Mostly because its plot was tough to follow, *The Burning Plain* flopped in theaters and received poor reviews. The *New York Times* said the movie didn't come "close to making sense." Still, Jennifer received favorable reviews for her performance. She also received a valuable lesson about filmmaking and life in general. She told the *Huffington Post*, "I learned that you can't have any expectations with life or with this business. *The Burning Plain* was a million-dollar movie with huge movie stars, and everybody was convinced that [it] was going to be huge and that was my star-making role."

Winter's Bone

In the end, *The Burning Plain* didn't turn out to be Jennifer's big break at all. And it didn't make her a household name. But Jennifer wasn't discouraged. She continued pursuing her acting dream with the same determination she always had.

Her next major move was to audition for successful indie film director Debra Granik. At the time, Granik was casting for her latest movie, *Winter's Bone*. Jennifer tried out for the lead role of Ree Dolly, a poor seventeen-year-old living in the Ozarks in

Missouri who takes care of her family and sets off on a quest to find her drug-dealing father. The film is based on a best-selling book called *Winter's Bone: A Novel* by Missouri author Daniel Woodrell.

Jennifer was one of two hundred people who auditioned for the part. She auditioned twice in Los Angeles and did not get the job. She believed it was because she was too pretty for the role.

But Jennifer wanted the part so badly that she didn't give up. She told the *Huffington Post* she "flew to New York like a psycho and showed up to the New York auditions with icicles in my hair and was like, 'Hi! I'm back!' I think that once they saw that I had the exact kind of stubbornness and competitiveness that Ree has, they were like, 'Oh, well, nobody else is going to be this stubborn and this crazy to embark on such a journey.'"

Director Granik said, "Jennifer was comfortable with the accent, and it made her reading really pop. For the first time I felt like I was really hearing Ree." Jennifer eventually won the role. Afterward, she moved back to Kentucky to reacquaint herself with the Southern dialect and Southern ways. She learned how to handle a gun, chop wood, and skin a squirrel. The *Winter's Bone* script required her to do all three of those tasks.

The last task listed—skinning a squirrel—later got Jennifer in a bit of trouble. In an interview, she told *Rolling Stone* magazine that the squirrel she skinned in the movie was real, which it was. What got her in trouble is when she spoke out harshly against a group called PETA. PETA stands for People for the Ethical Treatment of Animals. It is an animal-rights group that strives to protect animals from cruelty. The group believed that skinning a squirrel definitely qualified as animal cruelty. PETA's president, Ingrid Newkirk, responded to Jennifer's statement. She said, "...one day I hope she will try to make up for any pain she might cause any animal who did nothing but try to eke out a humble existence in nature."

Jennifer later further explained her role in the squirrel incident to TV talk show host Jimmy Kimmel. She said the squirrel was dead when she skinned it. She told Kimmel, "A hunter came over with a Ziploc bag full of frozen squirrels. We didn't kill them for the movie. The only reason we did it was because they were already dead."

When she was done in Kentucky, Jennifer left for southwest Missouri. That is where *Winter's Bone* was filmed. Jennifer rarely wore makeup during filming, had her teeth painted yellow, and intentionally didn't protect her lips from the weather so they would crack. She did it all to look more like her character. She wasn't too pretty for the role any longer.

Jennifer said filming in the Ozarks during the winter was hard work, especially because she was in every scene of the movie. She told *The Wrap*, "We had very little time, and we were working with harsh weather conditions. And there wasn't a single set on the whole film—it was all done on those locations. I remember getting tired and sick and calling my mom one night crying, telling her to come." Jennifer toughed it out and not only made it through filming, but she also excelled.

When *Winter's Bone* was released at the Sundance Film Festival in early 2010, audiences and critics loved it. It won the festival's top award. Then, it was released later that year in theaters across the country. The Sundance honor was just the first of many awards for the film.

As much as people liked the film, many people liked Jennifer's acting in it even more. *Rolling Stone* magazine said, "Her performance is more than acting, it's a gathering storm. Lawrence's eyes are a roadmap to what's tearing Ree apart."

Jennifer was nominated for more than two dozen awards for her role in *Winter's Bone*. She won several of them, too, including best actress awards from film festivals and critics in the United States, Canada, and Sweden. She was even nominated for a prestigious Golden Globe award. She told *USA Today*, "For the Golden Globes you get so excited. You get to dress like a princess and dress so beautifully and then by the end of all the fittings it's like 'gosh put me in something black that no one will make fun of me for.' There are so many different opinions and you start not trusting your own because it's the world that's going to be seeing it. You're dressing for a billion different people."

A Life-Changing Nomination

Soon, people began saying Jennifer's acting in *Winter's Bone* might even earn her an Academy Award nomination. When those nominations were announced in January 2011, *Winter's Bone* received four of them: Best Supporting Actor, Best Writing, Best Film, and a Best Actress nomination for Jennifer.

Jennifer was watching the announcements on TV with her family

Jennifer Lawrence ▶ was quite young when she starred in her critically acclaimed hit Winter's Bone. *This photo was taken at the Sundance Film Festival.*

when she heard her name called. She told *Access Hollywood*, "I kinda freaked out. I was jumping up and down, squealing, smiling, hugging my mom, I did the whole thing. I was just a cliché."

Jennifer's life changed dramatically immediately after her nomination. In some ways it changed for the better. Suddenly, she was one of America's hottest actresses. Her name was becoming better known. Roles that she once had little chance

This photo was shot as Jennifer Lawrence prepared to attend the Oscars, where she was nominated for her performance in Winter's Bone.

of getting were now within her reach. But Jennifer said there was also a downside to so many people knowing who she was.

During the hoopla leading up to the Academy Awards, she noticed the way people treated her had changed. She told the *Wall Street Journal*, "I got a taste of fame from the Oscars and I didn't like it. That's a terrible thing to say because it's such a tremendous honor. But I went from being normal Jennifer to being at these parties where I couldn't be the girl making dumb jokes in the corner. Everybody's treating me differently and talking to me differently and I know that they're lying and that they're sucking up to me."

Jennifer ended up losing the Academy Award to Natalie Portman. But that did little to lessen the pride she felt for the work she and others did on *Winter's Bone*. She told *USA Today*, "It's the only thing that really brings tears to my eyes. To think that we were working on this tiny movie. It was freezing cold and all of us were sick. And this was a tiny little movie but we were all there because we believed in it. I never imagined it [would become so popular] and that's what gives me goose bumps."

Jennifer didn't slow down after her Academy Award nomination. Instead, she began working harder than ever. She started being mentioned as a contender for what seemed like every high-profile acting job. She ended up working on three films that were released in 2011. The first, *Like Crazy*, was in many ways similar to *Winter's Bone*. It was also first released at Sundance. And it also won that festival's top prize. The film is a romantic drama. In it, Jennifer plays the role of Sam, a young woman who gets caught up in some adult situations with actor Anton Yelchin.

That same year, Jennifer also played Yelchin's love interest in *The Beaver*. That movie is a dark comedy featuring Mel Gibson and Jodie Foster. Jennifer said she learned a lot about life from Foster, who also had begun acting at a young age. Jennifer told the *Wall Street Journal* she learned by observing and talking with Foster. Jennifer said, "She's the only [big star] who I've seen who's just so normal. Every time I look at her I say a silent prayer, 'Let me end up that way.' I'm not worried about being nice. I want to be more than nice: I want to be normal."

After her great experience with Winter's Bone, Jennifer Lawrence was ready to take on even more movies.

Playing Mystique

Jennifer Lawrence's biggest role of 2011 was one in which she played a character that is nowhere near normal. She played a villain mutant named Mystique in the film *X-Men: First Class*. The movie was the latest installment in a series about superheroes. It took a lot of work to transform Jennifer into the scaly, blue Mystique character. Each day, six make-up artists worked on turning pretty Jennifer into scary Mystique. First, the artists put scales on her body. Then they airbrushed her, applied five layers of paint, and put yellow contact lenses in her eyes. The process took seven hours. It wasn't easy on Lawrence. One day, her skin became infected, and a doctor had to be called to the set to treat her. After getting in costume each day, Lawrence still had to act for a full day on the set. Afterwards, it took a few hours to remove all the makeup. It was an exhausting experience.

X-Men: First Class was filmed in England. Lawrence lived in London while she was there. She often hung out in the city with *X-Men* co-star Zoë Kravitz, the daughter of musician Lenny Kravitz.

She also struck up a relationship with another of her *X-Men* co-stars, British actor Nicholas Hoult. Rumors of the romance quickly spread, but Lawrence did not talk much about it to the media. She said she prefers to keep her personal life to herself. But that didn't stop gossip magazines and Web sites from reporting on the couple. They were

Jennifer Lawrence became fast friends with Zoë Kravitz (left), an actress who is the daughter of musician Lenny Kravitz. Here is Kravitz with Zoe Lister-Jones.

photographed together at several locations, and the pictures were published for the world to see.

Lawrence eventually confirmed that she was dating Hoult. She told *Glamour* magazine, "I don't find myself attracted to actors, which is a weird thing to say when you're dating one." She said she believes that "British men have these wonderful manners, and everything they say is funnier just because of the accent."

Lawrence is comfortable with the way she looks. She told *FLARE* magazine, "I don't really diet or anything. I'm miserable when I'm dieting and I like the way I look. I'm really sick of all these actresses looking like

For a time, Jennifer ▶ Lawrence dated British actor Nicholas Hoult.

35

birds ... I'd rather look a little chubby on camera and look like a person in real life, than look great on-screen and look like a scarecrow in real life."

People couldn't stop talking about Jennifer, especially when *X-Men: First Class* was released in June 2011. The film debuted at the top of the box office in twenty countries. But Lawrence didn't spend much time celebrating its success. She already had moved on to even bigger things.

The Hunger Games

Three months before the *X-Men: First Class* premiere, Lawrence had landed the biggest role of her career. She was chosen to star in the film version of Suzanne Collins's best-selling young adult book *The Hunger Games*. Winning the role wasn't easy. To get the job, Lawrence had to beat out many popular and successful young actresses, including Emily Browning, Lyndsy Fonseca, Chloë Moretz, Emma Roberts, and several others.

Lawrence won the lead role of Katniss Everdeen. Katniss is a girl who tries to save her sister by taking her place in a survival event called the Hunger Games in a dystopian future land that was once the United States. Author Collins, who also helped with the movie, said Lawrence was easily the best person for the role. She said, "Jennifer's just an incredible actress. So powerful, vulnerable, beautiful, unforgiving and brave. I never thought we'd find somebody this amazing for the role. And I can't wait for everyone to see her play it."

Fans of Collins's books couldn't wait, either. The anticipation leading up to *The Hunger Games* was enormous. Everyone believed the film was going to be a super smash, and Lawrence was going to achieve one of the highest levels of fame possible because of it.

Long before the movie was filmed, people were comparing *The Hunger Games* to the mega-smash *Twilight*. Lawrence tried her best to squash those comparisons. She told *Vanity Fair* magazine, "*Hunger Games* is not *Twilight*, and while I hear the comparisons, it's really premature to say that it will be the same phenomenon. ... If it does become a crazy phenomenon, I'll soak up my freedom now!"

In other interviews, Lawrence answered questions comparing her to *Twilight* star Kristen Stewart. Stewart is such a big celebrity that she is constantly harassed by paparazzi. Her every public move makes news somewhere. Lawrence told *Glamour* magazine, "I'd never want to be that famous." Two years earlier, Lawrence actually had tried out for two parts in *Twilight*, Bella Swan and Rosalie Hale. Stewart won the role of Bella, and actress Nikki Reed got the part of Rosalie. Not winning either of the parts may have turned out to be a blessing in disguise for Lawrence. Instead of working on *Twilight*, she went to work on *Winter's Bone*.

Lawrence had read *The Hunger Games* book before auditioning for the movie. She knew how big a deal getting the role could be. She knew it could change her life. So after she was offered the role, she took three days to think about whether she should accept it. Because there were three *Hunger Games* books, saying yes to doing one movie likely would mean committing to doing the other two when they were made. There was a lot at stake.

Lawrence told *Glamour* magazine, "I wanted to make sure I was ready for this. And I am. I feel like I got a ticket to another planet and I'm moving there and there's no turning back, and I don't know if I'm going to like that other planet or have friends there. It's just scary."

Preparing to Film

Once she said yes, Lawrence worked hard to prepare for her role. She learned to shoot Katniss's favorite weapon, a bow and arrow (she was taught by an Olympic medalist!), exercised every day, and

To promote The Hunger Games *film, Jennifer Lawrence and her two main co-stars, Liam Hemsworth and Josh Hutcherson, toured the malls of the United States. Here, she and Hemsworth sign autographs for fans.*

Jennifer Lawrence also appeared on the Late Show with David Letterman to promote The Hunger Games. Here she signs autographs outside the show's studio.

dyed her hair brown. After the filming was complete, she even took part in a mall tour to help promote *The Hunger Games*. During the tour, she and her co-stars, including Josh Hutcherson and Liam Hemsworth, visited cities across the United States. They met with fans, signed autographs, and answered questions.

The goal of the tour was to get people even more excited for the opening of the film. Jennifer told TV host David Letterman that on the tour fans would scream and cry. One girl even fainted when she saw Lawrence. The actress told Letterman,

"Some of them start screaming before they even make it to me then run away. They work themselves up." She said her favorite fans were the ones who would dress up like Katniss and then go into shock when they got to meet the person who played her. Lawrence said, "They look miserable. Won't look at me. Won't talk to me. ... If it weren't for their [costumes] I would think they hated me, that they didn't even want to be there."

The Hunger Games cast enjoyed working together. The young stars became good friends and even pulled pranks on each other. One time, Hutcherson got Lawrence good. He told *Entertainment Weekly*, "We have this fake dummy on set, this really gnarled-up scary-looking thing. The other day I put it in her bathroom in her trailer, and she told me she actually peed her pants, she was so scared. I'm sure she's going to pay me back. I'm just terrified because she's someone I can see taking it to the next level, and somebody could get hurt." Lawrence and her co-stars also went on adventures. One time, she, Hutcherson, and Hemsworth went to a small creek to catch crawdads. Lawrence told *People* magazine, "I saw [a crawdad] and was like, 'Catch it!'" Instead of grabbing a crawdad, Hutcherson accidentally grabbed a leech instead. It got stuck to his hand.

The Hunger Games was so highly anticipated that the location of the filming was kept secret for months. The movie was even filmed under a code name so no one could discover its location.

From left to right, Josh Hutcherson, Jennifer Lawrence, and Liam Hemsworth appear at the Los Angeles premiere of The Hunger Games.

When *The Hunger Games* was released in March 2012, it lived up to the lofty expectations. It broke attendance records across the world. Lawrence's star also rose. She appeared on countless TV talk shows and in magazines and newspapers. Critics also loved the film. They gushed about Lawrence's acting, too. *People* magazine said she was "... a fan's dream. With her soulful eyes and innate grit, she gives skilled hunter

Kristen Stewart (pictured) and Jennifer Lawrence often compete for the same roles.

Katniss equal doses of complexity and appeal. Forget *Twilight*'s insipid Bella Swan. *This* is a literary heroine girls can cherish."

Lawrence won an MTV Movie Award for Best Female Performance for *The Hunger Games*. The trophy she received was shaped like a golden box of movie-theater popcorn. Talk quickly began that she also might be worthy of another Academy Award nomination.

It eventually became known that *The Hunger Games* was filmed in North Carolina. When word got out, tourists began flocking to the area and visited sites where their favorite stars had been. Businesses based on *The Hunger Games* began to pop up, as well. One company even created a tour based on the movie. *The Hunger Games* phenomenon was nearly identical to the *Twilight* craze. During its opening weekend in the theaters, *The Hunger Games* even earned more money than any of the four *Twilight* films had. Lawrence may not have thought her latest movie was going to be as big as *Twilight*, but it clearly was.

Until the release of *The Hunger Games*, Lawrence had managed to keep her personal life somewhat private. Much of that changed with the release of that movie. Paparazzi began following her more. Tabloid magazines even tried to create a feud between Lawrence and Kristen Stewart. Lawrence told the *Los Angeles Times*, "Things like this tabloid war shouldn't stress me out, but it's kind of like being in high school when one friend says you said something bad about your other friend and you know you didn't say anything. It gives you a knot in your stomach. I'm afraid that's what it's always going to be like."

The two actresses weren't really fighting. However, they did continue to compete against each other for high-profile acting jobs. Both hot young stars, for example, said publicly that they wanted to win the lead role in the movie *Lie Down in Darkness*. The movie, scheduled to be released in 2014, is based on a 1951 book by William Styron. Both actresses wanted to play the part of Peyton Loftis, a young girl who commits suicide. Stewart told *Elle* magazine, "I want to play Peyton more than anything I can possibly taste or touch in my life. I want to play her so bad."

Lawrence had equally strong feelings. She said to *W* magazine, "I am obsessed with that part. I have this feeling of protectiveness over characters I want to play. ... If someone else gets the part, I'm afraid they won't do it right. I'm trying to write the director ... to convince him that I should be in his movie. I'll chase him if I have to. I'll sit outside his house." Unfortunately for Lawrence, Stewart eventually won the role.

Immediately following the release of *The Hunger Games*, it was announced that the second book in *The Hunger Games* trilogy was going to be turned into a movie. Lawrence began filming *The Hunger Games: Catching Fire* in Atlanta, Georgia, in September 2012. The movie was released in November 2013.

The reason fans had to wait so long to see *The Hunger Games* sequel is because Jennifer was spending a large portion of 2013 filming another *X-Men* movie, *X-Men: Days of Future Past*. The movie was based on one of the most popular storylines the *X-Men* comic books ever produced.

Before those two blockbuster sequels hit theaters, moviegoers were able to see Lawrence in a few other roles. She starred with Elisabeth Shue in the horror film *House at the End of the Street* and with Bradley Cooper and Academy Award winner Robert De Niro in the comedy *Silver Linings Playbook*.

In February 2013, at twenty two, Lawrence won the Academy Award for Best Actress for her performance in *Silver Linings Playbook*. The honor that she had lost out on when she was just twenty years old was now hers.

When she tried to walk up the stairs to the stage to accept the award, she tripped over her dress and fell. Best Actor nominee Hugh Jackman rushed to help her up, and she then began her speech to a standing ovation. She said, "You guys are just standing up because you feel bad that I fell and that's really embarassing. But thank you."

Despite her Oscar win, Lawrence still has big goals. She talked about her future with the *Huffington Post*: "When I think about myself in five years, sometimes I think about work and where I'll be in my career. But I normally just think about what kind of person I'll be. Will I be calmer or will I be more hyper? Will I learn how to listen or am I just always going to stay in this … zone

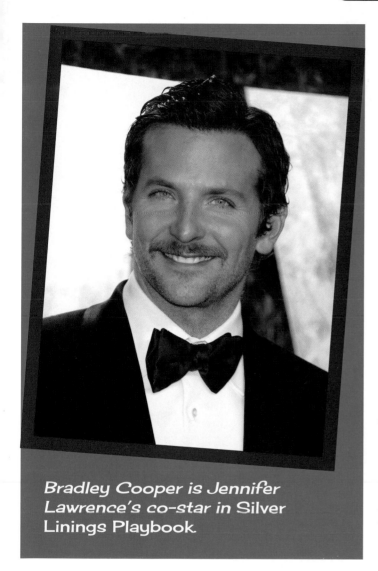

Bradley Cooper is Jennifer Lawrence's co-star in Silver Linings Playbook.

◄ *Jennifer Lawrence has a bright future in Hollywood.*

where I could just keep talking forever?" Lawrence has told many interviewers that she wants to live as normal a life as a big star can. Her fans love her because she's real in interviews and behaves like a normal person. She makes mistakes and often says silly things.

Lawrence's acting successes may have placed her under bright lights, but she still wants to be able to turn those lights off at the end of each day. As she told *Bang Showbiz*, "I see my future the same as I did when I was a little girl … having a family and being a mom."

Further Info

Books

Collins, Suzanne. *The Hunger Games* Trilogy. Scholastic Press: New York, N.Y., 2010.

Krohn, Katherine. *Jennifer Lawrence: Star of* The Hunger Games. Lerner: Minneapolis, Minn., 2012.

O'Shea, Mick. *Beyond District 12: The Stars of* The Hunger Games. Plexus Publishing, Inc.: Medford, N.J., 2012.

Internet Addresses

Jennifer's official Web site

<www.jenniferslawrence.com>

Jennifer's page at the Internet Movie Database

<http://www.imdb.com/name/nm2225369/>

Index

A

Academy Awards (Oscars),
   5–10, 29–31, 44–45
acting
   commercials, 20
   education, 12–14
   feature films, 32
   indie movies, 22–29
   modeling, 16–19
   as passion, 18–19
   reviews, 25, 28, 41–42
   role preparation, 26–27,
      38–39
   sitcoms, 20–22
   TV shows, 20
awards, honors, 5–10, 21,
   23, 28–31, 42, 44–45

B

Basinger, Kim, 24
The Beaver, 32
Bening, Annette, 6
The Bill Engvall Show, 20–22
The Burning Plain, 24–25

C

Churchill Downs, 11
Collins, Suzanne, 36

F

fans, 39–40
Foster, Jodie, 32

G

Garden Party, 22, 24
Gibson, Mel, 32
Golden Globes, 28

Granik, Debra, 25, 26

H

Hemsworth, Liam, 39, 40
Hoult, Nicholas, 34–35
The Hunger Games, 8,
   36–43
Hutcherson, Josh, 39, 40

K

Kentucky Derby, 11
Kidman, Nicole, 6

L

Lawrence, Gary, 12
Lawrence, Jennifer
   childhood, family life,
      11–16
   confidence, 14, 19, 25,
      35–36
   on fame, 31
   high school, 18
   social life, 34–35, 43
   work ethic, 18, 26–27,
      38–39
Lawrence, Karen, 12, 16
Lie Down in Darkness, 43
Like Crazy, 32

N

Newkirk, Ingrid, 27

O

Othello, 14

P

paparazzi, 37, 43
PETA, 27
The Poker House, 22–24

Portman, Natalie, 6, 8, 31

S

Silver Linings Playbook, 44
squirrel skinning, 26–27
Stewart, Kristen, 37, 43
Sundance Film Festival,
   28, 32

T

Theron, Charlize, 24
Twilight, 37, 42

W

Walden Theatre, 14
Williams, Michelle, 6
Winter's Bone, 5, 25–29,
   31, 37

X

X-Men: First Class, 8, 33–36